Becoming a Pioneer

Becoming a Pioneer

A Book Series

The Month-by-Month Guide
to Double your Business and
Take Over Your Industry in a Year

Bimal shah

Book 4: Capturing your Biggest Opportunities

Becoming a Pioneer - Book 4

ISBN: 978-0-9909014-7-1 Paperback

ISBN: 978-0-9909014-8-8 Hard Cover

RAJPARTH **ACHIEVERS**
— For the High Achiever in You —

TheOneYearBreakthrough.com

For more information, email: Bimal@theoneyearbreakthrough.com

Rajparth Achievers, LLC
5550 Glades Road, Suite 500
Boca Raton, FL 33431

Connect with Pioneers around the World. Every Month. With the book purchase, you are a member. No strings attached.

Join Me and walk away with personalized insights for you in the monthly Club meeting.

Get Your Free Membership here
https://bit.ly/ThePioneersClub

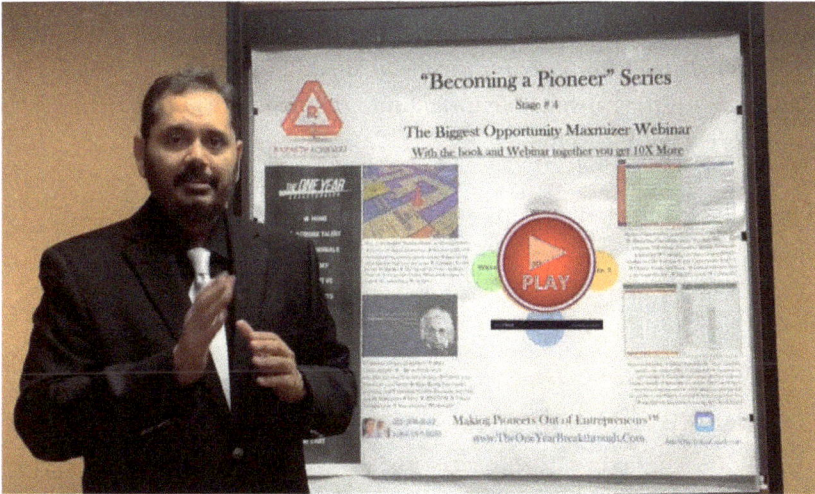

Learn Exponentially More.

This book is best used in conjunction with its training that allows you to not only capture your biggest opportunities but also secure your exponential growth through those opportunities.

Get Your Free Video Training at
https://bit.ly/TheOpportunityMaximizer

To my wife, Ami, and our daughters, Rajvi and Parthvi. This book would not have been possible without the efforts of Ami with the editing. Her strength and support are priceless. Also, I am indebted to my daughters for their invaluable insight into the structure and design. My family is everything to me.

I love them with all my heart.

Contents

Author's Preface

Making Pioneers! —The What and Why

What is a Pioneer?

A pioneer is unique and different from the rest.

To be a pioneer, you need to be the Only One at something. This book is about breaking all the barriers and obstacles you have in your life, work, habits, and mindset. The purpose of this book is to bring a 10x to a 100x transformation in your perspective about your own self—to assist you in realizing your true potential in a very short time.

Why be a Pioneer?

God has made every human being unique and different. When every human becomes unique and different, the whole world can work in harmony. Becoming a pioneer happens through stages and discoveries. I wrote this book with the intent to create the essential stages and discoveries you will need at each step. Drawing from my own experiences, it builds fresh perspectives that can take your business to the next level.

Editor Ami Shah with Author Bimal Shah

How To Get the Most Out of This Book Series

Go slow. This is a book you do not want to read fast. Write in the margins. Scribble in it, make notes, use sticky notes. Carry this book with you wherever you go. This is your book and customized manual to help you at least double what you believe you can do in a year.

Even if you answer one question from this book, it will have a positive impact on your life or business. Below are five ways you can make the most out of it:

1. Read first, think second, and then write: Read a sentence or two or a paragraph. Think about it and answer the questions that follow.

2. Go digging: Look up something in your business or your personal life related to the question. And then come back and answer the question.

3. Use Sharp Pencils with an eraser on top: Instead of using pens, please use pencils, as while you are writing your thoughts on the questions, the answers may change in due course.

4. Watch the video before you start reading: In the video, you will get a lot more insights into the book itself. It will walk you through powerful elements to scale.

5. Scan the QR CODE and save the QR CODE link in your Notes on your Smartphone: When you answer a specific question, look up the links listed in the Link Tree. See if there is a resource for the problem you are trying to solve. The Link Tree is very useful. It works like magic; you will find new and amazing things each time you look.

Special Advice for Using This Book
in Uncertain Economic Times

As we all know, the future is questionable. I recommend using this book series in a sequential order to stabilize and speed up your income growth. Follow the advice in the acronym UNCERTAIN:

U-Unique - Discover from each book how to become unique. Book #5 lists elements to leverage to be unique.

N-New – Apply the different tools and systems taught in book #1, book #9, and book #11. To bring in the new you in record time.

C-Confidence – Use the Confidence Journey tool from book #5. To build daily confidence in your journey.

E-Empathy – Use the Self-Empathy skills from book #10 and book #2 (this one). To deal with uncertainties, biggest pains, or frustrations.

R-Resilience – Lay the foundation for building resilience with a powerful vision in book #1. Apply the Book #12 resiliency skills.

T-Transparency – Discover from book #3, book #4, and book #6 how to use good or bad transparency. This is to propel you and your business to the next level.

A-Audacious – From book #1, book #13, and book #6 you will discover how to maintain and chase audacious goals.

I-Implementation – From Book #7 on Sprints and Book #8 on Leadership. Throughout each book in the series, you will become a master implementor.

N-Next Steps – Every single chapter in each book helps you build your customized next steps. There is no way you can't stabilize or grow if you follow all the steps you built by yourself, using this book series.

Special Advice for Using this Book Series
in Prosperous Economic Times

When times are good, you can make them better by using this book series with the acronym AWESOME as follows:

A-<u>Algorithms</u> - In business when there are a lot of opportunities coming your way, you need to apply an algorithm: a one-line business plan. Build your customized scale from algorithms listed in book #4 and book #13.

W-<u>Wins</u> – At the end of every chapter, you celebrate your wins. In book #5 you have the tools that make it a recurring habit.

E-<u>Extra</u> –There is no traffic beside you in the extra mile. In book #12, you will have the systems to drive on the no-traffic roads.

S-<u>Surprisers</u> –What to do when your team and customers surprise you. You are bound to get surprised quite often. Discover the best responses in book #1, book #2 (this book), book #3, book #4, and book #10.

O-<u>Omnipresence</u> –Through book #6 and book #3, you will build your own systems. Through book #11 you will build your own skill sets. Through book #9 you will build the platforms. In book #10 you will have the systems and tools to automate omnipresence.

M-<u>Multiplication</u> –When times are good, you need systems to multiply. Through Book #1 you will lay the foundation for multiplication. Through Book #7 you will build the skills. Through Book #8 and book #9 you will build the traits for becoming a multiplier and systems essential for it.

E-<u>Extinguishers</u> –When things are happening like rapid fire, you need a different kind of extinguisher. This is to extinguish the fires and keep up the pace you are moving at. Build your own fire extinguishers from book #4.

Introduction

This book was written with the intent to make an immediate positive impact on you, the reader. Hence, there are many questions, with valuable tools, resources, stories, and action steps.

This way, you can answer even one question and see a positive impact. I want you to take notes from this book. And that's why I left a lot of space for you. I want you to make this book your "own unique book."

There are many self-development and business books out there. But I wrote this one to direct your thinking in a specific way. So, sit back and relax while you read.

There is one topic in this book that allows you to go deep. It also helps to make a real positive difference in the least amount of time. Even if you spend five minutes reading this book, you will feel the transformation.

What's unique and different about this book is that it is a series you will cherish forever. It has your goals, your plans, your actions, and most of all a system you can use every year.

The system consists of a series of 13 stages. Each lasts 4 Weeks; you can achieve your 3-year goal in one Year. Besides, I did not want to write anything about something you already know.

Alongside the questions for you to answer are tools to use. And some practical solutions you can put in place and see great results.

I hope this book will make a positive impact on your life. For your convenience, I left you enough space to answer each question. I have noticed many people have bigger handwriting and need more space to write! I look forward to meeting you in Part V!

Week 1

Your Biggest Security Is Your Biggest Opportunities

I used to think that security is going after what you feel comfortable with and what you can do where there is little to no risk or difficulty. Now I know that looking for no risk is my temptation, as it is essential to realize why *capturing opportunity* is very important. This is my motto: "A pessimist looks at the glass half empty, an optimist looks at the glass half full, a realist would look at the glass with half air and half water, and an opportunity seeker will just take the glass and drink the water and feel good." So, taking advantage of opportunities is the only way to attain security and stability.

I used to be the same way. But in pursuing only the opportunities, I was familiar with, I didn't make enough progress. That's when I said to myself: *I must get out of this and chase the biggest opportunities, those that have big meaning, and not follow the money.* When I did that, the money followed. My mission followed. Now I am on a mission to make Pioneers out of Entrepreneurs by helping them achieve their three-year goal in one year that is closest to their 25-year vision.

What follows next is a series of questions, tools, exercises, and next steps to help you capitalize on your biggest opportunities.

It is essential to focus on the right opportunity and the biggest opportunities, as opportunities are everywhere, and they keep on coming—that doesn't mean you keep on chasing them. The first step is to answer the question below:

If you had a magic wand so that everything you wanted could come true, and **you could magically create your biggest opportunity**, and you were meeting yourself three years from today—and were to look back to today—what has to have happened with the biggest opportunity during that period, both personally and professionally, for you to feel that you had a meaningful transformation in your life and business? If there were a big blank white picture frame in front of you and you could wave the magic wand to see whatever picture you wanted to, what picture would have to be in the frame for you to feel a meaningful transformation?

Your Imaginary Ideal Biggest Opportunity:

Meaningful Personal Transformation:

_____
_____
_____
_____
_____
._____
_____

Meaning Professional Transformation:

_____
_____
_____
_____
_____
_____
_____
_____
_____
_____
_____
_____
_____

Once you've identified the three-year "Biggest Opportunity Vision," now identify the top five opportunities that exist that relate to your vision and make a list of them below.

1._____
_____
2._____
_____
3._____
_____
4._____
_____
5._____
_____

Discover whether the opportunities connect to your ultimate goals and vision. It's essential that the goals align properly. You can go a mile in a million directions, or you can go a million miles in one direction. The latter brings meaningful transformation.

Secondly, are these identified opportunities truly your biggest ones in terms of your goal? ❐ Y ❐ N

If yes, good job. If not, it's time to reflect deeply on your three-year vision, and where you see yourself going. Then identify which opportunities will help you get there. Once you've done this, you've identified your biggest opportunities.

Will these opportunities help you attain your three-year goal in one year? ❐ Y ❐ N

If yes, that is great. If not, then you have not identified your biggest opportunities. To truly answer the previous question, go back to it. When done, you will be able to tick yes to this question.

After revisiting the question, please write out what you think your biggest opportunities are that connect you to your goals and vision.

_____
_____
_____
_____
_____
_____
_____
_____
_____
_____

So, perhaps you identified *several* big opportunities. That is okay. My job here is to help you identify *which ones* truly are your biggest.

Also, sometimes what we think of as our biggest opportunities might not truly be that.

Probability, Possibility, and Profitability:

For something to realistically be your biggest opportunity, it needs to answer positively to three questions, *based on the probability, the possibility, and the profitability of the opportunity*. And other factors.

What is the probability that these opportunities will help you achieve your 3-year goal? (You are trying to discover if there is a 51 percent or higher probability.)

The *probability* of an event happening is the extent to which that event is likely to occur. The higher the probability, the greater the likelihood the event will happen. For example, you could be spending $20,000 on a 30-second TV commercial that would go to a mass audience. What is the probability of *your* audience watching it and taking action to generate sales? Your job is to decide at which times *your* audience is most likely to be in front of the TV; that will be the best time to air the commercial, as the likelihood of your ideal audience taking the required action will be higher. Therefore, you must think of your opportunities in terms of probability too. So, you can know the best time to take the required actions.

Think of probability as the likelihood—based on all the elements in your life and business at that moment—of you capturing that opportunity in the time frame you are looking at.

So, what are the odds that the biggest opportunities you listed will help you achieve your three-year goal?

Are the odds stacked in your favor? ❏ Y ❏ N

If yes, your opportunity has passed question one! Well done. You have successfully identified the three-year "Biggest Opportunity Vision," as well as the top five opportunities that exist that relate to your vision. And the probability of success is high. If not, then you need to identify opportunities that have a high probability of succeeding in helping you connect your ultimate goals to your vision.

What is the *possibility* that your opportunities will help you attain your three-year vision?

Possibility has to do with the ability to make something possible. It has to do with the scientific, systematic processes that it's possible to create or that already exist that can make your opportunities come into being. Is that opportunity something you can make happen? Also, when will it happen? What's the time frame it will take to happen?

So, it might be possible that your opportunities will help you achieve your dreams and goals. But *when*, in a year? Three years? Ten years? Take, for example, the case where you have a business contract that will bring your business to the next level, but the funds are spread across a three-year plan. This is a good opportunity—quite all right—but it won't help you achieve your three-year goal in a year. In addition, if the funds are spread over three years and the project consumes all your time and resources, how much money will you be left with to take home? That is where profitability also comes into play.

So, back to the question: Is it possible that your opportunities will help you achieve your three-year vision in one year? ❏ Y ❏ N

If yes, good job. One more question to go, and we can then safely establish that your identified opportunities are truly your biggest. If not, it's time to think deeply and look for an opportunity that will help you achieve your vision in three years. Because your opportunities must be the ones that can help you achieve your three-years vision in one year, or possibly less.

This book is mainly focused on your business opportunities, so profitability plays a big role. What is the profitability of your opportunities?

_____
_____
_____
_____
_____
_____

Profitability has to do with the degree to which a business or activity yields profit or financial gain. It is a measurement of efficiency, and ultimately the success or failure of an opportunity.

Also, profitability is the major goal of any business venture. You will agree with me that you won't want to do anything that will not yield profits.

Are your identified opportunities profitable? ❏ Y ❏ N

If yes, kudos. Those are great opportunities. If not, what will it take to make them profitable? Find options that make your opportunities profitable. If you can't, then you need to look elsewhere.

After going through the above questions, can you confidently say that the probability and possibility of your identified opportunities are very high—at a minimum more than 50 percent and at a high of more than 80 percent? Profitability must match or exceed your intended minimum net margins or dollar amounts.

If that's the case, then they are amazing opportunities—worth looking into. Please turn to the flowchart on the next page to understand the evaluation process for the biggest opportunities.

Flowchart for Biggest Opportunities

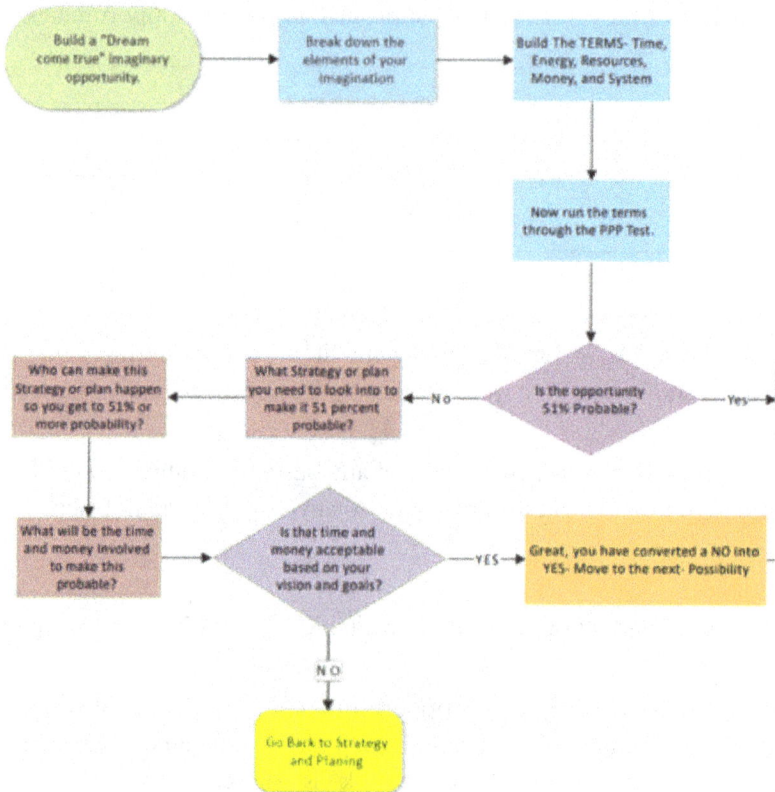

- Build a "Dream come true" imaginary opportunity.
- Break down the elements of your imagination
- Build The TERMS- Time, Energy, Resources, Money, and System
- Now run the terms through the PPP Test.
- Is the opportunity 51% Probable? — Yes→
- No→ What Strategy or plan you need to look into to make it 51 percent probable?
- Who can make this Strategy or plan happen so you get to 51% or more probability?
- What will be the time and money involved to make this probable?
- Is that time and money acceptable based on your vision and goals? —YES→ Great, you have converted a NO into YES- Move to the next- Possibility
- NO → Go Back to Strategy and Planing

Flowchart for Biggest Opportunities

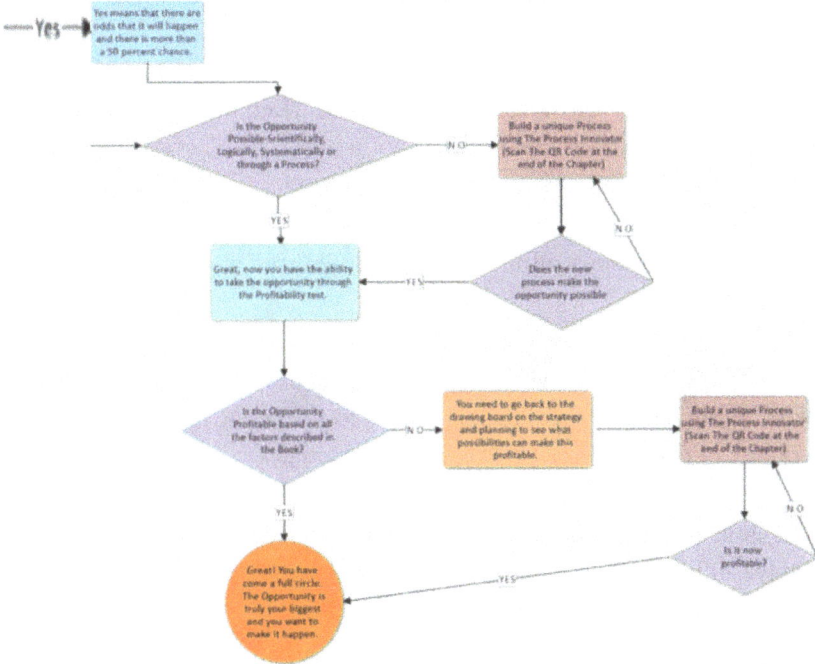

Yes means that there are odds that it will happen and there is more than a 50 percent chance.

Is the Opportunity Possible Scientifically, Logically, Systematically or through a Process?

NO → Build a unique Process using The Process Innovator (Scan The QR Code at the end of the Chapter)

YES

Great, now you have the ability to take the opportunity through the Profitability test.

← YES — Does the new process make the opportunity possible

NO ↑

Is the Opportunity Profitable based on all the factors described in the Book?

NO → You need to go back to the drawing board on the strategy and planning to see what possibilities can make this profitable.

→ Build a unique Process using The Process Innovator (Scan The QR Code at the end of the Chapter)

YES

Great! You have come a full circle. The Opportunity is truly your biggest and you want to make it happen.

← YES — Is it now profitable?

NO ↑

Besides the three Ps, you evaluated in the flowchart, there are other factors to consider. Let's look at them one by one.

What is the time factor of your opportunities?

_____
_____
_____
_____

The time factor of anything should always be taken into consideration, as time is a resource that plays an important role in the organizational and management process of a business venture.

Do your opportunities afford you time for yourself and your family?
❏ Y ❏ N

If yes, that's great. You will be able to strike a balance between life and work. If not, consider that it is unhealthy to not create time for yourself. You might need to reconsider these opportunities.

The time commitment of an individual when starting a business opportunity can be so great that it severely reduces the family time. And this can put a strain on your relationships.

What are the top 5 aspects of your life that these opportunities will take your time from?

1._____
_____
2._____
_____
3._____
_____
4._____
_____
5._____
_____

So, if the time factor is not so great, you will have to decide if it's a risk you are willing to take, or if you want to look for another opportunity that affords you time for your family.

Another factor to consider is money.

Will these opportunities take away your money?

_____
_____
_____
_____

Titus Maccius Plautus was a Roman playwright and philosopher. A phrase often attributed to him is, "You must spend money to make money." Today this is a popular phrase, and it is true. To have a profitable venture, you must invest a certain amount of money into it. But it also means that you don't have to spend a lot to make a lot. You must spend just the right amount (or less) of money to make what you need to. You can get to that right amount through research, experience, and—most importantly—expert advice. It can save you a lot of money. I have a target of 5X on the investment you make in the business, and that's why I provide a 5X guarantee to my consulting clients.

Will these opportunities put a financial burden on you?
❏ Y ❏ N

If not, then they are worth looking into.

If yes, is the opportunity worth the risk to you? ❏ Y ❏ N
If you can risk it, and you are sure the odds are in your favor and that if you put in the work, you will at least break even, then it might be worth the risk. If not, you need to consider other opportunities.

An opportunity for your business can sometimes mean you have to make a financial sacrifice until your business breaks even and the cash flow becomes sufficient to pay you a substantial salary. Sometimes, the financial sacrifices you must make can end up depleting your family's savings, putting their financial security at risk.

Is the financial risk so great that you think you should wait to have larger savings before venturing into it? ❏ Y ❏ N

It is not always a good idea to borrow money, as it can get you into much bigger problems than you can handle. On the other hand, the right structure and offer may make it very attractive. To discover if you should borrow or not, please visit https://bit.ly/TheDebtManagementSystem

Now that you have evaluated the risk and the debt opportunities, if the financial risk is greater than you can handle, this is not one of the biggest opportunities available to you to achieve your three-year goals in a year. In the opposite case, then it might be a viable opportunity to investigate.

After looking at all these factors, you must still consider asking yourself questions like:

Will these opportunities do something I haven't done before and make it better? ❏ Y ❏ N

If yes, then that's a good thing. There's always room for improvement. If not, I leave you with these unforgettable words of dire warning about rat races and hamster wheels: "Insanity is doing the same thing over and over again but expecting different results."

To help you identify if these opportunities will be repeating what you have been doing previously, make a list.

What are the top 5 things that you are currently doing with your business?

1._____

_____
2._____

_____
3._____

_____

4._____

_____

5._____

_____

After making this list, review the opportunities you laid out and identify what are the top 5 things that these opportunities will address in your business.

1._____

_____

2._____

_____

3._____

_____

4._____

_____

5._____

_____

Once you make the above list, you want to verify that the opportunities address the current problems in your business. Understand that problems are like puzzle pieces and unless you find the missing pieces of the puzzle, you can't solve the problem.

Do the identified opportunities address the current issues in your business? ❏ Y ❏ N

If yes, that's great. You are ready to move to the next chapter. If not, you must go over the exercises again until you identify the opportunities that address the top issues in your business currently. The reason is any problem not resolved in the business only gets bigger over time in the business and harder to resolve.

Kudos on completing the exercises and answering the questions this week. In week two I will teach you about executing your biggest opportunities, for increased business prosperity. But before heading off to week two, please check out the next page, where you will have the chance to write the takeaways from this chapter that can assist you in building SMART Goals; they will greatly facilitate your success.

Week 1

Your Chapter Takeaways

What are your top 5 biggest PROBABLE, POSSIBLE, and PROFIT-ABLE OPPORTUNITIES?

1._____

_____

2._____

_____

3._____

_____

4._____

_____

5._____

_____

What is THE ONE opportunity you need to work on in the next 90 Days that will help you get closest to your three-year biggest oppor-tunity?

_____

_____

_____

_____

_____

Useful Resources

QR Code to scan and get all FREE Tools and Resources:

Link from the QR Code:

https://linktr.ee/TheOneYearBreakthrough

Link to all my events:

https://www.eventbrite.com/o/bimal-shah-7943115300

Time to Celebrate

Before you move to the next chapter, take time to celebrate.

Here are five little ways you can celebrate:

1. Find Suspense Movies on Amazon Prime that have an IMDB rating of 8.0 or more (a great find—you'll enjoy it).
2. Play with your dog or pet.
3. Cook the most unusual dish.
4. Do jumping jacks until you can do no more.
5. Call an old friend you haven't called in years.

Week 2

SMART KASHFLOW for Your Biggest Opportunities

Many times, I've identified golden opportunities and big opportunities but got stuck in the execution phase of getting them to the finish line. Now I know that executing and getting an opportunity working is where you need the right mindset, tools, and systems.

I used to be in the same boat, where execution would seem an impossible task and I'd want to throw up my hands and give up on the opportunity. Then I said to myself there had to be a better way. Think about this—writing 13 books that walk you step by step through achieving your three-year goal in one year. That is like climbing Mt. Everest. So, I put several systems in place to make it happen. What I realized in the process is that it is all about focusing on getting it done and becoming SMART—you would be surprised at how I define SMART Goals . . .

Below I would like to walk you through a series of mindset exercises, tools, and the next steps to becoming the master of getting it done.

Being able to sustain growth and be profitable is never guaranteed in the business world. Technological and scientific advances shorten the life cycles of products and services. Business models change, and new competitors appear from outside the industry. This constant change makes it necessary to seek new opportunities.

Next, let's move to how to analyze your identified biggest opportunities in terms of each function of the business.

Will these business opportunities affect people? ❑ Y ❑ N
If you ticked no, think again; everything influences people? If yes, will they affect them positively or negatively?

How will your employees be affected?

_____
_____
_____
_____
_____

Business opportunities can lead to more jobs in the short or long term. Take, for example, a sales company that is expanding; to handle the large influx of orders, more hands will be needed.

Will these business opportunities challenge existing firms to be more competitive? ❑ Y ❑ N

If not, then they might not be promising opportunities. Everyone wants to have a piece of the next big thing in any industry.

If yes, how do you plan to have an edge over your competitors?

_____
_____
_____
_____

There are a lot of brands doing similar things. But at the end of the day, you still have a favorite brand. Why? Because there is something, they do that you like. That is the edge your favorite brand has over others.

The fastest way to build that edge is to become the only company in your industry; to do that, you need to combine why you do what you do with how you do it. For example: "We are on a mission to make pioneers out of entrepreneurs by helping them achieve their three-year goal in one year." Make your mission your tagline. For example: "Making Pioneers Out of Entrepreneurs"—That's my why and my tagline, or slogan.

Why do you do what you do?

_____
_____
_____
_____
_____
_____
_____
_____
_____
_____
_____
_____
_____
_____

What is a unique result you deliver that allows you to make your WHY come true?

_____
_____
_____
_____
_____

How will you deliver that unique result?

_____
_____
_____
_____
_____

When money comes easily, we typically tend to make fast financial decisions; as a result, money goes away fast. Therefore, it's wise to approach building your business as if you have minimal resources. To do this, write a business plan for yourself to "*make* money for you" and "not to *get* money for you" (a loan or equity).

Many start-ups fail because of this very reason: their business plan is written to get loans or investor funding, not to make money; and precisely for that reason, they don't get funded, as the evaluators or investors aren't able to understand how the business is going to make the targeted amount of money.

Money comes from cash flow more than investor funding or debt. One of the biggest reasons companies and businesses fail is cash flow. If there is a heaven and hell in business, it is cash flow. When you have cash flow, you feel like you are in heaven. And when you don't, it feels like hell.

Along with the execution of a strategy is the disbursement of cash for the execution to take place. To achieve this, identify your cash flow in terms of numbers. It could mean a fixed monthly figure that allows you to meet obligations plus set aside for growth.

What is your cash flow?

_____
_____
_____
_____
_____

According to a study performed by Jessie Hagen of U.S. Bank, "82 percent of businesses fail because of poor management of cash flow." That's a high rate of failure for a system that can be controlled easily." ForbesWomen, Dec. 22, 2020. To avoid falling into this trap, identify your negative cash flow in terms of numbers.

What is your negative cash flow?

_____
_____
_____
_____
_____

Yes, cash flow can be negative. This happens when, in the hope that your revenues will pick up and one day exceed your expenses, you consistently spend more than you make. That hope is not a strategy. Set a deadline for when you will stop spending more than you make.

With that in mind, how do you intend to avoid negative cash flow?
1._____
_____
2._____
_____
3._____
_____
4._____
_____
5._____
_____

In a negative cash flow system, the money coming into your business is way less, compared to the large sums leaving it. With positive cash flow, your business can sustain and grow to the next level in a year. The next step is to define cash flow in terms of your own business.

What is your positive cash flow?

_____
_____
_____
_____
_____

A *positive cash flow* means you can let your revenues decide your expenses and not vice versa.

How do you intend to make sure your business always has a positive cash flow?

1._____

_____

2._____

_____

3._____

_____

4._____

_____

5._____

_____

Think of ways in which these business opportunities would help you build a positive cash flow.

How will your business opportunities affect your cash flow?

_____

_____

_____

_____

_____

If the business opportunities will affect your cash flow negatively in the short run and long run, they are not your biggest opportunities to help you leap into achieving your three-year goal in a year.

With negative cash flow, you may think it is impossible to achieve your three-year goal in one year. Now I am about to let you in on a little secret called "KASH-FLOW for Cash Flow." This can help you generate cash flow even if you are having negative cash-flow.

This is how you generate cash flow in your business, even if you lack capital or reserves or are even dead broke. Please keep reading . . .

K A S H

K	_Knowledge_ - Applied Knowledge is Power- Seek knowledge that is aligned with your imagination.
A	_Attitude_ - Improve your attitude and you make more money.
S	_Skills_ - Become THE EXPERT in your CRAFT- become the only one.
H	_Habits_ - Improve your habits and improve your cash flow.

F L O W

F	*Finish* - Finish one thing, as the biggest issue is entrepreneurs take important projects to a finish line.
L	*Leverage* - Leverage what you've GOT and what you can GET- Leverage your current resources plus available resources - Focus on what you have vs what you don't have.
O	*Omnipresence* - Look for Opportunities that allow you to be Omnipresent for your customers.
W	*Win* - Winning every day is essential. Target and Achieve Three to Six BIG Victories Daily,

Now that you know how to generate cash flow without having money to do so, let's look at how your opportunities make you competitive.

How will your business opportunities challenge existing firms to be more competitive?

Every business opportunity with a favorable return on investments will always have competitors lurking around. For example, we have Pepsi competing with the Coca-Cola brand.

Next, we will look at the strategy aspect of your business.

How will these business opportunities affect your business strategy?

A *business strategy* is a set of clear goals, plans, and actions that outlines how a business will compete in a particular market. The three keywords are "goals" first, "plans" second, and "actions" third. So, the important thing is to think of what these opportunities will do for your business and plan accordingly.

Will these business opportunities affect your current business strategy?
❏ Y ❏ N

If not, you must think again. Every opportunity will always affect the way you do things. It can be either positive or negative.

Will these opportunities affect your business strategy negatively?
❏ Y ❏ N

If not, then the opportunities are favorable. If yes, you need to rethink. Every opportunity is supposed to help you leap towards your goals.

How are you going to plan your business strategy with these given opportunities?

A *business strategy* is essential for any company that is seeking to grow strategically. So, with growth comes the need for revising your strategy. Preparing a business strategy requires strong skills in business analysis and strategic planning, as well as a good understanding of several functions—for example, sales, marketing, and distribution.

What are the top 5 things you would take into consideration when planning your business strategy due to the expansion opportunities?

1._____
_____
2._____
_____
3._____
_____
4._____
_____
5._____
_____

Keep in mind that when you plan a business strategy for expansion, several factors (the market you want to expand into, your competitors, and your company's structure, strengths, weaknesses, etc.) come prominently into play. Also, your strategy should be flexible enough to handle change.

So, after the business strategy, what next? It's *the execution.*

Do you have the plan to execute your strategy?☐ Y ☐ N

If yes, kudos, you are on track toward achieving your goals. If not, you need to get on it. You can delegate it to other members of your team, and you review it for approval.

For an entrepreneur, strategy and execution go together. Your strategic skills will allow you to create policies, establish direction, and determine how to effectively allocate resources to achieve your goals, while execution involves practical and tactical skills needed to put a plan in motion.

How do you intend to execute your business strategy?

_____
_____
_____
_____
_____
_____
_____
_____

Bahaa Moukadam, the founder and head coach at SeeMetrics Partners, said during an interview in September 2014 on the radio show *Money Talks*, "A lot of organizations put great strategies together, but they don't follow through." He went on to say that "eighty percent of organizations fail at the execution part of the strategy." Yahoo News September 2014.

To systematically execute your strategy, there are stages or structures to follow or apply. I am going to provide one structure that you can use. Divide your strategy into four parts—25 percent each—and target 80 percent progress for each part.

Now that you have some direction on execution, what are the steps you'll take to ensure the successful execution of your strategy?
1._____
_____
2._____
_____

3._____
_____
4._____
_____
5._____
_____

An execution done right is a disciplined process. Making the strategy work involves you, the entrepreneur, undertaking a logical set of connected activities.

Do you set clear priorities? ❏ Y ❏ N

If not, work on establishing clear priorities, as most entrepreneurs might fail in carrying out their strategy if they set too many priorities. If yes, that's good, as establishing only one clear priority at a time with supporting initiatives has a higher probability of completion.

Do you collect and analyze data? ❏ Y ❏ N

If yes, keep up the good work; this is key to ensuring the proper execution of plans. Collecting data will help you stay on top of things, as you will be able to evaluate what's working, and you can enhance that to boost performance. If not collecting and analyzing data, you need to get started on it.

Do you have periodic meetings with your team? ❏ Y ❏ N

Periodic meetings are essential, as, without continuous communication, employees can lose touch with your goals and objectives.

If you and your team don't have periodic planned meetings, make plans towards starting. If yes, kudos. Also note that it is recommended to end each meeting with a review of what was decided, who's responsible for delivering what, and when it should be delivered. Create this review at the meeting and send it out to all employees by mail, so the important points are kept at the top of your mind.

Do you evaluate the success of your strategy?❏ Y ❏ N

If not, you need to do so; that way, you can know the progress made and where to improve on it. If yes, remember there's always room for improvement. You can put in measurables for the success of your strategy and answer the next question.

How do you evaluate the success of your strategy?

1. _____
_____
2. _____
_____
3. _____
_____
4. _____
_____
5. _____
_____

As part of the process of evaluating your strategies, be sure to meet with your key management personnel periodically to evaluate the progress of the strategic plan. At these meetings, aim to exploit the company's strengths and opportunities while mitigating weaknesses and threats.

How will your business opportunities affect your cash flow?

_____
_____
_____
_____
_____

If the business opportunities will affect your cash flow negatively in the short run and long run, then they are not your biggest opportunities, that will help you leap into achieving your three-year goal in a year.

Any business opportunity that will enable you to have a positive cash flow, in the long run, will have to affect the sales of your company positively.

How will these business opportunities affect your sales?

Every entrepreneur wants to make sales. And with the opportunity for expansion, it should be your desire to increase your sales. So if these opportunities would not affect your sales positively. It's not something you should be looking into.

Next, let's look at marketing because if you desire more sales, you need to put the effort into your marketing.

How do you market your products?

Marketing refers to all activities a company undertakes to promote the buying and selling of its products and services.

What forms of marketing do you currently engage in?

1._____

2._____

3._____

4._____

5._____

There are several different marketing strategies that will likely drive more sales. They include different forms of advertisement, affiliate marketing, and so on.

What other forms of marketing would you engage in, with an increased marketing budget?

1._____

_____

2._____

_____

3._____

_____

4._____

_____

5._____

_____

Will these business opportunities enable you to increase your marketing budget? ❏ Y ❏ N

If yes, those are great opportunities, as you will get to increase your sales and move closer to achieving your goals. If not, how then are you going to increase your sales? Good opportunities should open avenues to increase your sales and enhance or expand other aspects of your business operations.

How will these business opportunities affect your business operations?

_____
_____
_____
_____
_____
_____

Business operations are activities that businesses engage in daily to increase the value of the enterprise and earn a profit.

Would these business opportunities help you optimize your business operations? ❏ Y ❏ N

If yes, then they are opportunities worth looking into. If not, then they may not be the right opportunities for you.

How would these business opportunities help you optimize your business operations?

1._____

_____

2._____

_____

3._____

_____

4._____

_____

5._____

_____

Your biggest business opportunities should be able to help you optimize all aspects of your business operations so that you can generate enough cash flow to cover your expenses and earn a fortune for yourself.

How would your business operations evolve as your business grows?

1._____

_____

2._____

_____

3._____

_____

4._____

_____

5._____

_____

Business operations evolve as the business grows, and together with your management team, you should plan to accommodate the changes to prevent glitches from occurring in the system. For example, as your business grows, you must be ready to handle arising challenges such as marketing or legal and capacity issues because if the business does not evolve with the changes in business operations, glitches such as omissions and errors will come into view.

With the expansion of a business comes the need for emerging technology and innovation.

Do you think your business needs technology? ☐ Y ☐ N

If not, think again because the role of technology in business is vital, as it provides a better way to manage your business. If yes, that's awesome.

In what ways do you need technology in your business?

1._____
_____

2._____
_____

3._____
_____

4._____
_____

5._____
_____

Technology has a big impact on your business operations. No matter the size of your company, technology can help you increase revenue and produce the goods your customers demand. Technology is changing many areas of business, such as communication, accounting, sales, data collection, logistics, security, and marketing.

What role does technology play in your business?

The major role of technology in any business is to drive growth and improve operations. And so, your biggest business opportunities should have plans for business expansion.

Do you currently have the technology necessary for efficient business operation and expansion? ☐ Y ☐ N

If yes, that's great. You can now move on to innovation. If no, make a list below of the top one to five technological platforms or software, or resources you need to have a base of efficient business operations and expansion.

1._____
_____

2._____
_____

3._____
_____

4._____
_____

5._____
_____

Will your business opportunities bring about innovation? ☐ Y ☐ N

If yes, that's the way to go because innovation brings about more avenues for growth. If not, then they are not business opportunities. Innovation drives growth.

How will these business opportunities bring about innovation to your business?

1._____
_____

2._____
_____

3._____
_____

4._____
_____

5._____
_____

Daily, the business world is becoming more technological, and innovative ideas are springing forth. As innovation nurtures business and since technology creates the way for it, we can say that to be sustainable, a business needs technology. So your biggest opportunities must include advancement in technology and innovation. Now let's look at what ties all aspects of a business together, Leadership.

How will these business opportunities affect the leadership of your company?

Leadership provides direction. It involves showing workers how to effectively perform their responsibilities, and it also involves the regular supervision of workers to ensure the completion of their tasks.

Will these business opportunities lead to a rearrangement in the order of control, and is that in your company's best interest?

An expansion in business sometimes comes with a rearrangement of roles, and the creation of new roles. Keep in mind that leadership also refers to the tone a company's management sets in terms of the corporate culture. If the rearrangement in leadership will bring about a change to your already established corporate culture, and it's not something you are comfortable with, then the opportunity is not one of your biggest opportunities that will help you achieve your goal.

Charles Kettering, who holds 186 patents, is widely attributed with saying, "There exist limitless opportunities in every industry." In other words, opportunities are everywhere; you just must be on the lookout.

On the other hand, opportunities can be missed, and therefore I highly recommend using a tool I created that will help you track opportunities. It is called The Daily Opportunity Tracker.

According to Thomas Edison, as quoted in An Enemy Called Average, "Opportunity is missed by most people because it is dressed in overalls and looks like work."

This tracker will be of great help to you, so you don't miss out on wonderful opportunities.

The Daily Opportunity Tracker™
Prepared For_____

No.	Name or Description Of The Opportunity	What is the end result they want that you can Deliver to them?	By When?	Why is it Important to them and Why is it Important to you?
1				
2				
3				
4				
5				

The Daily Opportunity Tracker™
Prepared For_____

What is the biggest obstacle that stands in the way of getting that end result?	What are one to three steps you need to take today to overcome that obstacle or make progress towards that end result?	
	1	
	2	
	3	
	1	
	2	
	3	
	1	
	2	
	3	
	1	
	2	
	3	
	1	
	2	
	3	
roduced in any way shape or form without the written		

The daily tracker will help you identify smart opportunities. Below is the definition of *smart opportunities* according to Indeed Career Guide and generally everywhere else on the internet.

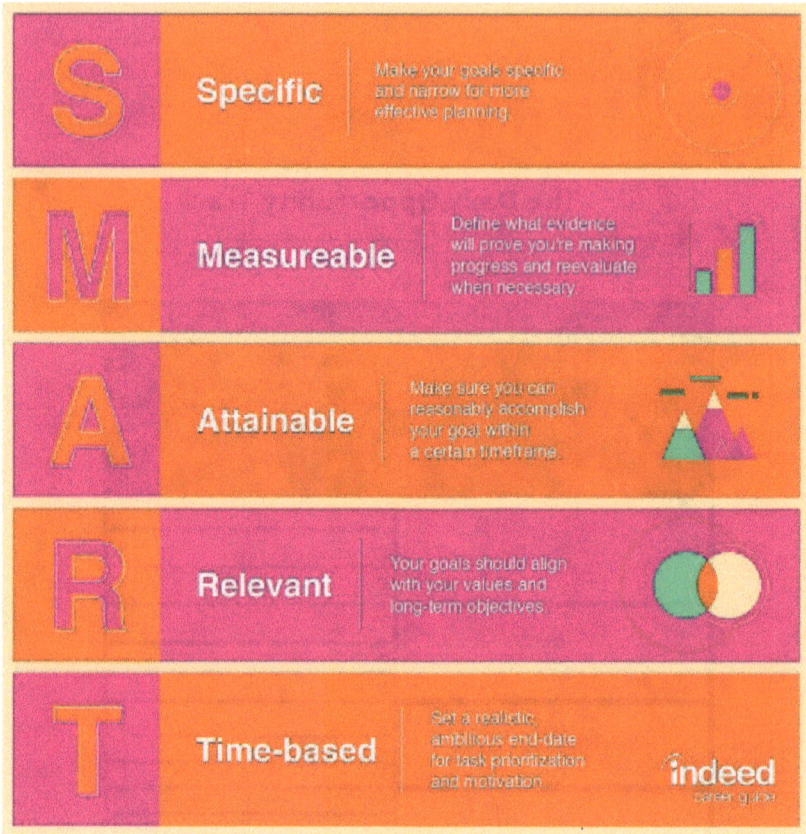

I believe the definition of the above goals puts you in a box and doesn't let you explore your true potential. It doesn't make you become limitless or infinite, yet every human has that potential. So, I have my definition of SMART Goals that is the complete opposite of the above.

My definition of SMART Goals.

S	SCARY	Goals should be scary and get you off your butt, making you work towards something meaningful.
M	METHODICAL	Goals should be methodical and allow you to build a new system that brings meaning for you and others.
A	ATTRACTED TO.	You should be attracted to and gravitate to these goals; they should pull you towards them.
R	RELEVANT	Your goal should be relevant to who you are as a person and your highest self.
T	TRUTHFUL	Your goal should be true to the time you are in and the time it will take. It should be truthful to you and to those for whom you aspire to attain them.

Do the goals you defined meet my definition of SMART?
☐ Y ☐ N

If yes, that's great. If not, please work on the question from the very first chapter of the book and get it to SMART.

Congratulations on completing the exercises and answering the questions this week. In week three I will teach you how to know if your opportunities are worth pursuing. Before heading off to week three, please check out the next page, where you will have the chance to write the takeaways from this chapter that can assist you in building SMART Goals. Once you have SMART Goals, you are ready to move into the next chapter.

Week 2

Your Chapter Takeaways

What are your top 5 biggest KASH FLOW Strategies to capture the biggest opportunities to achieve your SMART Goals?

Write your answer as follows:

My (KASH FLOW) strategy of _ will help me capture _ (the biggest opportunity) to achieve my goal of _ (Your SMART Goal)

1._____
_____

2._____
_____

3._____
_____

4._____
_____

5._____
_____

Useful Resources

QR Code to scan and get all FREE Tools and Resources:

Link from the QR Code:

https://linktr.ee/TheOneYearBreakthrough

Link to all my events:

https://www.eventbrite.com/o/bimal-shah-7943115300

Time to Celebrate

Before you move to the next chapter, take time to celebrate.

Here are five little ways you can celebrate:

1. Do Ten Burpees.
2. Watch a sports game that you don't know much about.
3. Watch a sports game that you love.
4. Go for a pedicure.
5. Take a nap on your favorite sofa in your house with your coziest blanket and pillow.

Week 3

Clearing Your Resurfacing Doubts

Even after you have gone through many strategies and exercises that were explained in the earlier chapters, some lingering doubts may still keep resurfacing in your mind.

Our minds never do let go of a resurfacing doubt unless it is cleared. That's what used to happen to me. Even if I forgot a particular doubt, it somehow resurfaced. So, I asked myself a question: isn't there a way and system to quickly analyze that doubt and move forward? Many a time, I used to find myself spending a lot of time in the analysis of the opportunity and even forgetting the lost-opportunity cost of the time I spent on it. So, I developed a system for clearing resurfacing doubts. For example, I would get a resurfacing doubt that started with several what-if . . . scenarios. There is no end to the what-if scenarios. Let me share a story.

It was such a recurrent problem for me, and I couldn't afford the wasted time. I had to be able to quickly analyze an opportunity, decide on it, and capitalize on it. So, I developed a system of asking myself a series of questions at checkpoints and conceived of some thinking tools. Now I have more than 200—that helped me answer the fundamental question: *Why is this doubt resurfacing back into my mind?*

Below, I walk you through a series of questions, exercises, tools, and next steps to help you build a system in place to answer the question when the need arises.

On a scale of 1 to 10, how happy are you with the current profitability of your business? (1 being the least and 10 being the most but could have room for improvement) _____

Regardless of what number you answered, going through the questions below can help you clear any resurfacing doubts.

What are the top three-to-five-line items in your P&L Statement you are most unhappy about or you believe you would like to improve?

1._____
2._____
3._____
4._____
5._____

How would the opportunity you are pursuing improve one or more of the line items above?

_____
_____
_____
_____
_____
_____
_____

Quite frankly, the only way to know the answer to this question is to assign people, systems, or strategies beside each of those line items and see if that helps you.

Who will help you improve the line items?

_____
_____
_____

What are the top three outcomes they need to deliver to improve those line items on your P&L?

1._____

_____

2._____

_____

3._____

_____

What are the top three systems you need in place to improve those line items on your P&L?

1._____

_____

2._____

_____

3._____

_____

How will you get those systems structured, set up, or installed?

_____

_____

_____

_____

_____

_____

Now we must analyze the strategy to clear that resurfacing doubt or doubts and give you confidence in your strategy. Behind every strategy, there is a story we tell ourselves. Below are the questions you need to ask yourself.

What is the story behind your strategy that is making those doubts resurface? (Example: Do the doubts relate to a prior experience you had, or did you hear it from someone, or did you read it somewhere, or do you have a gut feeling about this, or you have never done this before and are afraid to dive in?)

How is the story you are telling yourself relevant to the current opportunity?

How is the current opportunity different and unique from the story that is creating the doubt?

After you have realized the uniqueness of the strategy apart from the story that is creating the resurfacing doubt, the next step is to get clarity on the execution of the strategy. Lack of clarity creates the final doubt about the strategy.

We are going to divide the success of the strategy into four milestones of 25 percent each and get clarity on those milestones.

What would be the first 25 percent milestone you need to achieve in the execution of the strategy to see meaningful progress through it??

What would be the second 25 percent milestone you need to achieve in the execution of the strategy to reach meaningful progress beyond the previous 25 percent milestone?

What would be the third 25 percent milestone you need to achieve in the execution of the strategy to see meaningful progress beyond the previous 25 percent milestone?

What would be the fourth 25 percent milestone you need to achieve in the execution of the strategy to see meaningful progress beyond the previous 25 percent milestone?

The next step is to convert these milestones into Projects, People, and Time.

Milestone 1:

No	Project	People (Team)	Estimated Time

Milestone 2:

No	Project	People (Team)	Estimated Time

Milestone 3:

No	Project	People (Team)	Estimated Time

Milestone 4:

No	Project	People (Team)	Estimated Time

Now that you have got all the projects, people, and timelines for your strategy identified, identify the money aspect with each of the projects.

This may require some research; you may even want to give the task to someone who can get you the estimated range of costs.

For any project where cost or money is an obstacle, go back to strategy and devise a different execution plan.

On the next page I've provided a table to help you assess the total investment needed for the opportunity

No.	Project	Estimated Investment Range	Milestone #	Feasible? Y/N	Next Step
TOTAL					

Once you've analyzed the breakdown of the costs and the total, compare that to the profitability you derived earlier. Ideally, you would like the profitability to be 5X. But it could be that the profitability is derived 5X or higher over the long term, as the costs may be one-time but the returns recurring.

Whatever the ROI (Return on Investment) is, you want to calculate the estimated rough ROI by the improvement you estimate to generate in the five key line items identified earlier.

What is the estimated improvement in the five key P&L (Profit & Loss) line items identified earlier?

No.	Line Item	$ _____ Improvement	Investment	Net Profitability
1				
2				
3				
4				
5				

Once you've done this, build a P&L statement specific to the opportunity to see the net profitability.

Opportunity Profit & Loss Statement		
Description	Amount	Total
Opportunity Revenue		
Less: Cost of Goods (Material & Other- Estimated Project Cost)		
Less: Cost of Goods Sold (People Cost – Time spent)		
Less: Pro-rated General business expense (from your business P&L)		
TOTAL NET OPPORTUNITY PROFIT		

Now you have the net opportunity profit. But no business opportunity is complete without knowing the personal impact on your income. Because of this opportunity, what would be your total income?

What are the additional freedoms you can buy because of this additional income? (Yes! Freedom can be bought, and happiness can be bought with money: going on vacations, buying your favorite car, or having the income you need to get the home of your dreams, etc.)

_____

_____

_____

_____

This may sound bizarre and funny at the same time. Many a time in my experience with different people and entrepreneurs, one of the things I've heard is that "I don't want to make more money because I have to pay more in taxes."

The good news is that it's not so bad, and there are ways to lower your taxes by talking to your tax advisor and accountant intelligently. To do that, you first need to understand—using the tax tables—how much income-tax deductions you need to fall into the tax bracket you want. Below are questions that will assist you:

Your Income *before*: _____

Your Income Tax based on the table next page: _____

Your Income after the opportunity: _____

Your Income Tax after the opportunity: _____

Net Increase: _____

Total Income Tax deductions you need to get the Income to where you would like to: _____

Below is a link to resources to lower your taxes:
https://bit.ly/LowerMyTax

I highly recommended that you consult with your CPA or other tax advisor to see what you need to do to reduce your taxes. The information provided above and on the next pages is just purely for your reference and information. Your situation and results may vary.

You want to take the number you calculated above to discuss with your accountant or tax advisor and see what's recommended.

Please see the tax tables on the next page . . .

2022 Tax Computation From the IRS 2022 Tax Tables

Section A—Use if your filing status is **Single**.

Taxable income. If line 15 is—	(b) Multiplication amount	(d) Subtraction amount
At least $100,000 but not over $170,050	× 24% (0.24)	$ 6,164.50
Over $170,050 but not over $215,950	× 32% (0.32)	$ 19,768.50
Over $215,950 but not over $539,900	× 35% (0.35)	$ 26,247.00
Over $539,900	× 37% (0.37)	$ 37,045.00

Section B—Use if your filing status is **Married filing jointly** or **Qualifying widow(er)**.

Taxable income. If line 15 is—	(b) Multiplication amount	(d) Subtraction amount
At least $100,000 but not over $178,150	× 22% (0.22)	$ 8,766.00
Over $178,150 but not over $340,100	× 24% (0.24)	$ 12,329.00
Over $340,100 but not over $431,900	× 32% (0.32)	$ 39,537.00
Over $431,900 but not over $647,850	× 35% (0.35)	$ 52,494.00
Over $647,850	× 37% (0.37)	$ 65,451.00

Section C—Use if your filing status is **Married filing separately**.

Taxable income. If line 15 is—	(b) Multiplication amount	(d) Subtraction amount
At least $100,000 but not over $170,050	× 24% (0.24)	$ 6,164.50
Over $170,050 but not over $215,950	× 32% (0.32)	$ 19,768.50
Over $215,950 but not over $323,925	× 35% (0.35)	$ 26,247.00
Over $323,925	× 37% (0.37)	$ 32,725.50

Section D—Use if your filing status is **Head of household**.

Taxable income. If line 15 is—	(b) Multiplication amount	(d) Subtraction amount
At least $100,000 but not over $170,050	× 24% (0.24)	$ 7,664.00
Over $170,050 but not over $215,950	× 32% (0.32)	$ 21,268.00
Over $215,950 but not over $539,900	× 35% (0.35)	$ 27,746.50
Over $539,900	× 37% (0.37)	$ 38,544.50

Kudos on completing the exercises and answering the questions this week. In the next week, our topic will be the concept of "making it up to make it happen," where you can build your dream business into a reality. Before heading off to week four, please check out the next page, where you will have the chance to write the takeaways from this chapter that can assist you in building SMART Goals.

Week 3

Your Chapter Takeaways

What top 5 biggest resurfacing doubts in your customers' minds will you convert into opportunities for you?

1._____
_____
2._____
_____
3._____
_____
4._____
_____
5._____
_____

What are the milestones you need to set to capitalize on those opportunities?

1._____
2._____
3._____
4._____
5._____

Useful Resources

QR Code to scan and get all FREE Tools and Resources:

Link from the QR Code:

https://linktr.ee/TheOneYearBreakthrough

Link to all my events:

https://www.eventbrite.com/o/bimal-shah-7943115300

Time to Celebrate

Before you move to the next chapter, take time to celebrate.

Here are five little ways you can celebrate:

1. Order your favorite dessert through Uber Eats.
2. Make a surprise visit to your welcoming neighbor.
3. Surf for some of the most beautiful places to travel in the world.
4. Practice karaoke
5. Dance with your better half.

Week 4

Making It Up to Making It Happen

Now that you have cleared your resurfacing doubt, it is time to "make it happen."

There are two more stages before your dream happens. You have to make it up (using your imagination), and you have to make it real (with a blueprint or project). And then you make it happen (through execution).

I used to wonder how geniuses go from making it up to making it real to making it happen. There is a journey and a process. In this chapter, I am going to share with you a system of building your imagination to the point where you see it working. This is a system that has been used successfully repeatedly.

Just like you, I have a lot of imagination and want to do things but saw that just imagining alone doesn't help. You must take the next steps. So, at first, I decided to just get started on something. You probably know that things in motion stay in motion. I know when I was writing this book series, it was just a figment of my imagination and then I started working on a daily system. That's not enough. You need a system, a structure to make it happen, and take it from imagination. I have now built that and share some of the features in this chapter.

A multimillion-dollar story I can share is about building a new business avenue for a client. This client was always wondering how to get into a new avenue of business without an astronomical start-up cost and make a lot of money. So, I asked him three questions that built a multimillion-dollar business with minimal investment for him:

1. What is the easiest thing to print on the badges? His answer—the alphabet and numbers.
2. Do you have the space, money, and resources to print those badges? His answer was an astounding, "Hell, yeah!"
3. Who would want to buy badges with just alphabets and numbers? His answer: "We already know 10 of them. We are getting started tomorrow."

This started the journey of building an additional $2.5 million business in less than a year.

Below I walk you through a series of questions, exercises, tools, and the next steps to help you go from imagination to making it real to making it happen.

The very first stage is to make sure your imagination is in alignment with the 25-year long-term vision and 5-year Moonshot that my Book no. 1 helps you build. Our brain can imagine so many things that the imagination must align with your long-term vision and Moonshot.

What are all the things you imagine when you look at each of the five biggest opportunities you've identified so far?

1._____
_____
_____
_____
2._____
_____
_____
_____

3._____
_____
_____
_____

4._____
_____
_____
_____

5._____
_____
_____
_____

How is each of the imagined things in alignment with your vision and moonshot?

1._____
_____
_____
_____

2._____
_____
_____
_____

3._____
_____
_____
_____

4._____
_____
_____
_____

5._____
_____
_____
_____

Now that your imagination is in alignment with your vision, the next step is to make sure it is in alignment with the 3-year goal you set. There is a difference between Vision and Goals. Your vision is what you foresee in terms of pictures; your goal is what you write in specifics like numbers. For example, your vision might describe the multimillion-dollar company of your dreams, but your goals might describe how many customers you ideally want to make the money you targeted in a year.

The next step is to take those five biggest opportunities and verify that they are in sync with your goals.

How is each of the five biggest opportunities in alignment with the "SMART" Goals you listed earlier?

1._____
_____
_____
_____

2._____
_____
_____
_____

3._____
_____
_____
_____

4._____
_____
_____
_____

5._____
_____
_____
_____

Now you've completed the "make it up" phase, and everything is in alignment. The next phase is to make it real. "Make it real" consists of scientific, logical systems and processes and gets technical in nature. This allows you to visualize what you're aiming for and believe that it's possible. Many entrepreneurs follow their dreams without a system and process. When they fail, they say, "Failure is part of learning and I tried." That is not effective. And the failure was destined to happen from the get-go, as you didn't have a structured system or process.

So, in this phase, we will build a system that first converts your "wants," or SMART Goals, into Needs. When your Wants become Needs, the structure and systems you build are much more effective than if you just chase your Goal as "Wants." After that we will look at how to capture the opportunities and make them real. To do this, it is imperative to understand from your perspective the purpose behind chasing the right opportunities.

The wants-and-needs analyzer will help you analyze what you want for your business, your time, your relationships, your money, and your purpose and how to get there. It makes you reflect on your current needs, and wants; then it's time to reflect on the next steps to take.

You can use the same tool to convert your goals and your wants into your "Customer's Needs" as well. This allows you to build an effective system or process after recognizing how to convert "Your Wants" into "Your Customer's Needs." All you need do is replace the word "Your" with "Customer" on the tool and answer the questions. It's that simple.

Please check out the tool on the next page:

The Wants-Needs Analyzer™

Prepared For_____ Date:_____

Your 3-Year WANTS	Your Current SITUATION	Your Cost of Inaction (Consequences) CoI	Your True CURRENT NEEDS
			For Your Business
			For Your Time
			For Your Relationships
			For Your Money
			For Your Purpose-Your BIG WHY

The Wants-Needs Analyzer™

Prepared For_____ Date:_____

RAJPARTH ACHIEVERS

Your Essential BREAKTHROUGHS	By WHEN	NEXT STEP

produced in any way shape or form without the written

The next step is to build a scientific system, or process. Every process has a beginning, a middle, and an end. Most of the chaos and fires happen in the middle. It is not fun being in the middle. More than 80 percent of the time, the reason the chaos happens in the middle is because you didn't begin right, or you didn't have clarity about the end result or hadn't worked hard and smart enough to define the end result correctly.

Let's begin by understanding the process of building and then build the "Make it Real" phase of capturing your biggest opportunities.

HOW DO YOU GET YOUR BEGINNING RIGHT?

In this stage, keep coming back to the beginning after you have understood all the problems in the middle and see how you can eliminate them by beginning right

BEGIN WITH THE END IN MIND

Spend enough time until you are absolutely clear about the end result for your process, your customers, and your business. Once this is clear, go to the beginning.

HOW DO YOU GET YOUR MIDDLE RIGHT AND AVOID ALL THE FIRES?

The middle consists of several stages or steps. This is where the majority of the time the chaos happens. Follow the fist formula identified on the next page to understand how to get the middle right and each stage or step in the middle right. The middle looks something like this. Whenever you discover problems in the middle, go back to the beginning.

Now that you understand the foundational framework of the process, it is time to go deeper into each step or stage and get those right. You get those right with the hand and fist formula.

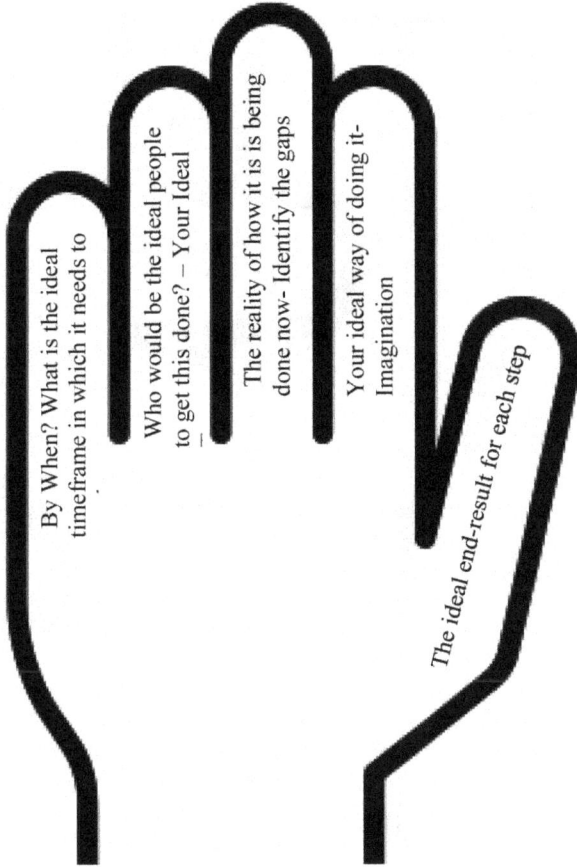

By When? What is the ideal timeframe in which it needs to

Who would be the ideal people to get this done? – Your Ideal

The reality of how it is is being done now- Identify the gaps

Your ideal way of doing it- Imagination

The ideal end-result for each step

The Hand Formula

Now we will apply the fist formula to your process to make sure your process has superpowers.

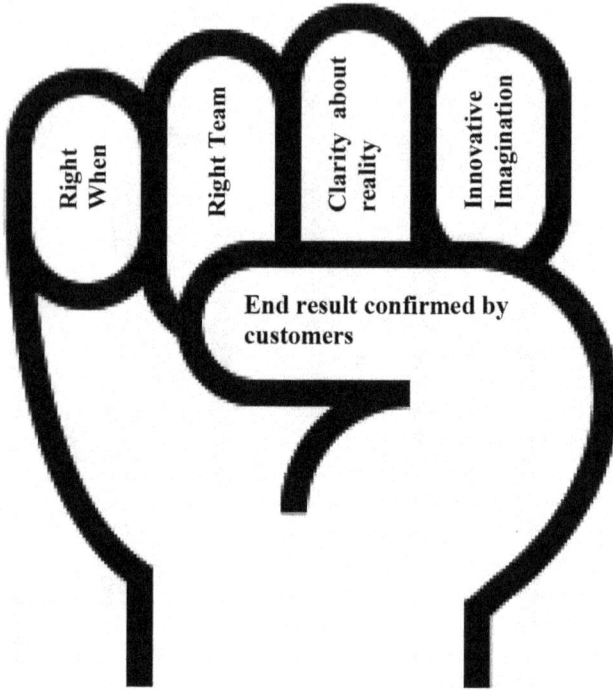

Right
When

Right Team

Clarity about
reality

Innovative
Imagination

End result confirmed by customers

The Fist Formula

You've Got the Superpower!!

Now that you have the superpower right in your hands, go ahead and build your first process below:

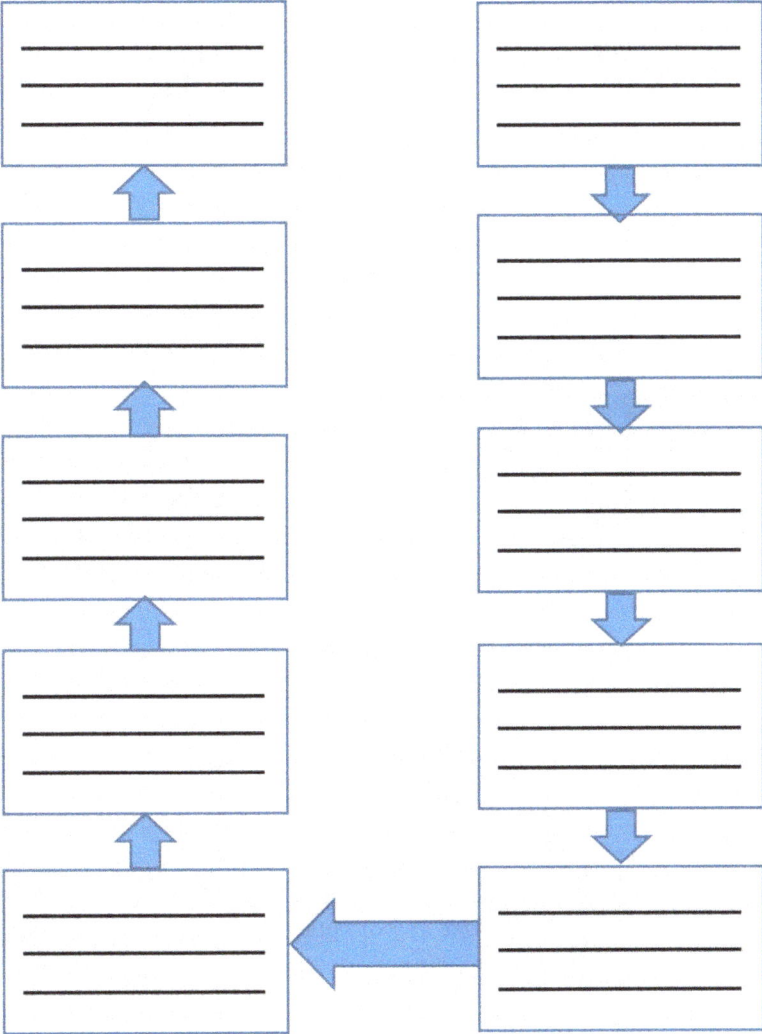

You don't have to have this many steps or go through these many stages. The fewer, the better. If it is more than 12 steps, revisit the process and see if there is anything you can eliminate. Give this process a name: "The _____ _____."

Now that you have "Made it Real," it is time to "Make it Happen." The secret of making it happen lies in making "The Weekly Sprint" successful, week after week. The key to making it successful is being proactive and not reactive.

You want to break down the process into minute steps and tasks and assign deadlines to each in the weekly sprint. The tool link is on the next page, and if you prefer a digital format, you can access it at https://thepioneers.academy/

You can incorporate these weekly outcomes into any of the platforms you use: Monday, Slack, Teams, Trello, Zoho, SalesForce, Asana, or something similar. If you aren't sure about what these are, you can utilize the Free Tools and Resources to evaluate your technology platform needs.

The next stage is "Make it Happen." You may meet challenges in this phase—the execution phase. If you have a team in place, it is essential that you've built a great company culture.

Do you have a great company culture? ☐ Y ☐ N

Do you believe that your culture needs NO improvement or changes? ☐ Y ☐ N

If you answered YES to both questions, you can move on straight to the Weekly Sprint Tool and schedule weekly outcomes for the next 4 to 12 weeks using that tool.

If you answered NO to any one or both questions, please have your team click the link and send their confidential responses to this tool.

https://bit.ly/TheCultureBuilderTool

You will then receive a free confidential analysis of the responses of your team. These responses will remain confidential with me; your team can be rest assured that only positive outcomes for the company will happen from their responses.

The biggest mistake entrepreneurs make is a reactive approach to tasks versus a proactive approach to outcomes. Never have a task, always an outcome. Have a list of outcomes to achieve day by day and week by week.

An *outcome* is different from a *task*, and you always in any task want to look for the outcome, defining the outcome rather than the task. For example, "Call Mr. Smith for an appointment" is a task. "I need you to set an appointment with Mr. Smith and I must meet with him this week, as I need to pick up a check to continue the project; otherwise, there will be no workers available to do the job in view of the labor supply issues. Do what you must to set an appointment with him by the end of this week." This is an outcome.

Having a proactive approach toward outcomes can make all the difference in the execution phase and "Make it happen" for you.

Please utilize "The Weekly Sprint" tool, which is designed to do "proactive outcomes" every day in your business.

The Weekly Sprint™

Prepared For_____

Results that you want to Achieve	Who?	What Specific Action needs to be taken to achieve that result?	By When?	Review Date?

The Weekly Sprint™

Prepared For_____

What are the obstacles, opposition or challenges you faced?	What Solutions will you implement to overcome those?	Result Achieved and By When

not be reproduced in any way shape or form without the written

I applaud you for completing all the exercises and answering all the questions in this book. You have learned how to capture your biggest opportunities, and you're prepared to take on the business world in style.

Please build the takeaways from the chapter on the next page and check out the free resources; they will assist in keeping your scalability sustainable.

Week 4

Your Chapter Takeaways
What are your biggest FIVE aligned "Making it up," "Making it Real" and
"Making It Happen" takeaways?

1. Making it up (Innovative Imagination):

_____
_____

Making it Real: (Process Name: The _____ _____): _____
_____

Making it Happen (Project Name: The _____ Project):
_____

2. Making it up (Innovative Imagination):

_____

Making it Real: (Process Name: The _____ _____): _____
_____

Making it Happen (Project Name: The _____ Project):
_____

3. Making it up (Innovative Imagination):

_____

Making it Real: (Process Name: The _____ _____): _____
_____

Making it Happen (Project Name: The _____ Project):
_____

4. Making it up (Innovative Imagination):

_____

Making it Real: (Process Name: The _____ _____): _____
_____

Making it Happen (Project Name: The _____ Project):
_____

5. Making it up (Innovative Imagination):

_____

Making it Real: (Process Name: The _____ _____): _____
_____

Making it Happen (Project Name: The _____ Project):
_____

Useful Resources

QR Code to scan and get all FREE Tools and Resources:

Link from the QR Code:

https://linktr.ee/TheOneYearBreakthrough

Link to all my events:

https://www.eventbrite.com/o/bimal-shah-7943115300

Time to Celebrate

Before you move to the next chapter, take time to celebrate.

Here are five little ways you can celebrate:

1. Take off a 3-day vacation at a local resort. Just pack your bags and leave with the family.
2. Order a surprise family portrait from one of the pictures.
3. Go to a place that makes the best smoothies and load up.
4. Read a novel.
5. Go for an evening stroll at the beach.

Doubling Your Business and Taking Over Your Industry in a Year!
Hidden Insights from this Book

Below, I have provided proven uncharted bottom-line insights from this book to double your business and rise in your industry in a year:

1. Your Biggest Security Is Your Biggest Opportunity:
Look for the biggest opportunity, not from how much you can make, but the biggest difference you can make for one customer. There is very little competition at the higher levels. You can easily double your business, working at that level. It will also make you unique—the only one—if you develop a unique process to solve their unique issues.

2. SMART KASHFLOW for Your Biggest Opportunities
A SMART KASHFLOW strategy for your biggest opportunity is to look at a customer-funded business model instead of an equity- or debt-funded business. Structure your business in a way that you are not dependent on debt or equity, and your customers can help you double your business and become the only one in it.

3. Clearing Your Resurfacing Doubts

Regularly look through your customers' eyes and see what doubts may be resurfacing in their minds. Eliminating those doubts can lead to multiple revenue opportunities for your business or revenue streams. This is a very unique way to double, convert their doubts into opportunities, and become the only one.

4. Making It Up to Making It Happen

Imagine and innovate the ability to overpromise and overdeliver (compared to your competitors). You would be surprised how quickly you become the only one and even see doubling your business as very feasible. Use "making it up to making it happen" with the "Super-powered fist" process to make the impossible possible!!

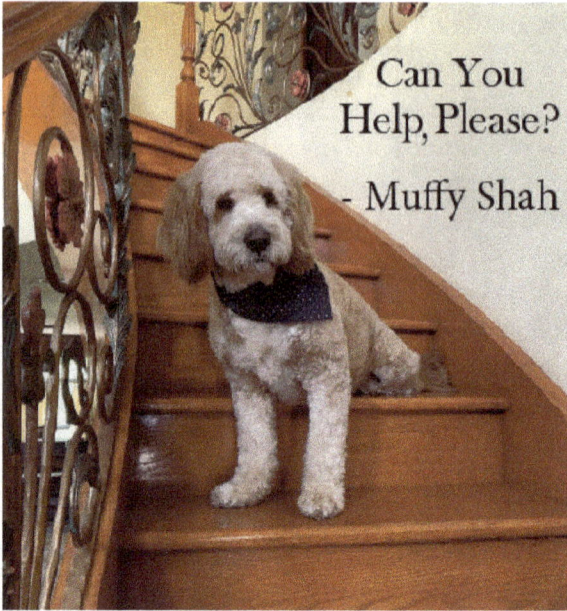

Can You
Help, Please?

- Muffy Shah

Thank You for Reading My Book!

I really appreciate your reading this book!

I would love it if you can give me an honest review.

I need your input to make the next version and my future books better.

Please leave me a helpful 5-Star review on Amazon, letting me know
what you thought.

Thank you so much!
—Bimal Shah

Please don't forget to check out the next book—on leveraging your biggest strengths and managing your weaknesses.

This is the next step in the sequence of steps to Becoming a Pioneer by achieving your three-year goal in one year.

See you in book 5!

DON'T FORGET

Join The Pioneers Club for FREE!

With the purchase of each book, you are Eligible to Join the Club Meeting for FREE

Connect with Pioneers around the World—Every Month. With the book purchase, you are a member. No strings attached.

Connect with Me and walk away with personalized insights for you in the Club meetings held every month on Wednesdays at 6 PM EST.

Walk away with a customized 30-Day Action Plan at each meeting.

Get Your FREE Membership at: https://bit.ly/ThePioneersClub

Conclusion

Dear Friend, we have come to the end of this book. If used appropriately, it will help you capture your biggest opportunities.

The book asks profound questions, which make you think. Please take time to reflect on each question and use the guides appropriately. They will help you take the transformational leap you want in your business, thereby helping you achieve your three-year goal in a year.

It is my utmost desire that I have given you everything in this book that will help you reflect on what you want and help you identify and capture your biggest opportunities in life and business.

See you in book five.

About the Author

Bimal Shah is an accomplished Senior Executive, Entrepreneur, Advisor, Coach, and Results Leader with more than twenty years of success in the financial services industry. Leveraging extensive experience in growth, entrepreneurship, talent development, financial reporting systems, profitability systems, and processes to scale, he is an asset for companies spanning various industries, sizes, and stages of growth that are seeking expert assistance in bringing their business to the next level. His broad areas of expertise include executive coaching, strategic planning, operations management, scaling, and growth.

As a breakthrough coach, Bimal has successfully helped companies generate growth of more than 50 percent in a year and has taken twenty-six companies to exponential growth in a year. Through his unique hiring process technique, he has helped dozens of companies hire highly qualified C-Level employees. He has worked with more than fifty companies, providing coaching and financial consulting services across an array of industries, including manufacturing, distribution, home health care, communications, security systems, and professional services. His unique Coaching-Planning-Accountability system has generated favorable results in record time for CEOs, reducing their working hours, in six months, by 35 percent.

As a result, CEOs see exponential company growth within a year, can hire smart and productive team members at all levels within a few months, and receive the tools to develop effective "out of the box" marketing strategies.

Bimal is also the founder of Rajparth Advisory Group (2005), which provides financial consulting services to entrepreneurs. From 1996 to 2005, before founding Rajparth Group, he worked as an independent advisor through Northwestern and New York Life, helping more than 1000 families preserve their assets, reduce their taxes, increase their income, and create everlasting legacies.

During his tenure, he was awarded the highest honor in the industry, The Million Dollar Round Table—Top of the Table Award for six years in a row and Global Corporate Award for Best Life Insurance Agent in the Asian Indian Community.

Bimal has also authored and published *The Daily Happiness Multiplier*, available on Amazon and in bookstores throughout North America. His unique "Success Deck" consists of 52 Workshop Videos and Tools to positively impact anyone's personal and professional life with a single tool each week for 52 weeks. Bimal earned his Bachelor of Commerce in Economics from the University of Mumbai and his Bachelor of Science in
Advertising from the University of Florida. He holds a Chartered Financial Consultant, Chartered Life Underwriter, and Certified Advisor in Senior Living from the American College at Bryn Mawr, Pennsylvania.

Some Accolades for Bimal's Work

"Bimal is the big picture guy and he takes us really deep. I might concentrate on one idea that I think is the greatest idea in this world, and Bimal will come back with making us think 10 times bigger and he's got this amazing ability to see opportunity. He lays out a great plan to get to where you want to go and makes it just so attainable. Every entrepreneur with big goals should consider hiring Bimal and if I could have Bimal in my pocket and carry him around at all times that would be great."
—*Mike Barnhill, Managing Partner, Specialist ID*

"Before, I was working 70–80 hours a week. Now it is down to 45–55 hours a week. The personal impact of his coaching has allowed me to spend more time with my family. The financial impact has been priceless because of the time saved. If you are struggling, consider hiring Bimal. His books and coaching have helped me plan and organize where I want the business to go. Bimal has also taught me to push my limits and think about things more in detail on why I am doing this."
—*Reginald Andre, CEO, Ark Solvers, Inc.*

"Bimal's books and workshops have further reinforced and enhanced some aspects of my leadership; in that, he has brought on a fresh perspective on my role as a leader of the company. In

addition to Bimal being a very engaging and energetic personality, he also has an open-minded and unique perspective to making learning a fun-filled experience for my staff, which then adds immeasurable value to my company."
—*Terry Sgamatto, Managing Regional Director, Seeman Holtz*

"I recently took a leap of faith . . . one that required a consistent amount of convincing myself out of a scarcity mindset and making an investment. It has just been a few weeks and I am very happy with the results of my decision. Under the advisement of Bimal, I have had to make some drastic decisions in my company but have to say overall, even though some were painful, they have all been results-driven and not emotional. I truly appreciate all that Bimal has helped me create in the first few weeks and cannot wait to see what comes next."
—*Sarah Martin, CEO, Experience Epic, LLC*

www.ingramcontent.com/pod-product-compliance
Lightning Source LLC
Chambersburg PA
CBHW060933220326
41597CB00020BA/3815